The Joy of Becoming Like Jesus

A Discipleship Manual

Discipleship 101

Spirit Life Ministries International

"...a foundation for many godly generations..."

Spirit Life Ministries International

The Joy of Becoming Like Jesus
Copyright © 2001 by F. Dean Hackett, Ph.D.

This title is also available as an ebook. Visit www.fdeanhackett.com/store

Requests for information should be addressed to Spirit Life Ministries Publications, Hermiston, Oregon 97838

───────────────────────────────────────

ISBN: 978-1539997078

───────────────────────────────────────

All rights reserved. No portion of this publication may be reproduced in a retrieval system, or transmitted in any form or by any means – electronic, mechanical, photocopy, recording, or otherwise – without the express prior permission of Spirit Life Ministries Publications, with the exception of brief excerpts in magazine articles and/or other reviews.

Front cover design: Stephanie Eidson
Back cover design: Aaron Hackett
Cover photography: Pixabay
Interior Design: Rosilind Jukić

Printed in the United States of America

I gratefully dedicate this work to my spiritual father, Reverend Edward L. Murphy. He is a man of impeccable integrity and Christ-like example, who patiently and lovingly discipled me and "equipped me for the work of the ministry"

Table of Contents

Introduction 6

What is a Disciple 9

What is a Disciple – Student Handout 11

Discipleship is More Than Excitement…It is Responsibility 13

Discipleship is More Than Excitement…it is Responsibility – Student Handout 17

Dealing with Myself and the World - Four Levels of Conflict 21

Dealing with Myself and the World -Four Levels of Conflict – Student Handout 25

My Body...an Instrument of Righteousness 30

My Body...An Instrument of Righteousness – Student Handout 32

Becoming Like Jesus by Rebuilding My Thought Patterns and Transforming My
Thinking 34

Becoming Like Jesus by Rebuilding My Thought Patterns and Transforming My
Thinking – Student Handout 40

Refocusing the Emotions and Redirecting the Will 48

Refocusing the Emotions and Redirecting the Will – Student Handout 52

The Secret of True Success in Life...Christian Meditation 55

The Secret of True Success in Life...Christian Meditation – Student Handout 57

Dealing with Temptation 60

Dealing with Temptation – Student Handout 62

A Disciple's Love Life 64

A Disciple's Love Life – Student Handout 66

Living a Life Filled with Joy 69

Living a Life Filled with Joy – Student Handout 71

Discipleship is Being a Servant 74

Discipleship is Being a Servant – Student Handout 78

Me and My Tongue 80

Me and My Tongue – Student Handout 82

Living in The Power of a Clear Conscience 84

Living in The Power of a Clear Conscience – Student Handout 85

A Key to Great Faith...Understanding Authority 87

A Key to Great Faith...Understanding Authority – Student Handout 90

Introduction

Jesus Christ was having one of His last conversations with the disciples before returning to Heaven. He had arranged this meeting with the eleven in a special mountain location of Galilee. He wanted to impress upon them, one more time, the critical importance of their future work and of the mission God was entrusting to them. When the eleven arrived at the meeting place they began worshipping the Savior, although, some still doubted His resurrection and were very much in question of their future.

"All power is given unto Me, in heaven and on earth..." – Jesus began. He continued: *"Go and make disciples of all nations, baptizing them in the Name of the Father and of the Son and of the Holy Spirit"*[1]

The fulfillment of that command became the passion and the vision that has impacted the world for two millenniums and has changed the very course of history. The impact upon Jerusalem was so dramatic in the early months the leaders declared, *"Behold, you have filled Jerusalem with your doctrine"*.[2] The vision to fulfill Jesus' command continued growing over the months and years after His ascension, reaching greater and greater masses of the Roman Empire. One city declared, *"These that have turned the world upside down are come hither also"*.[3] The Great Commission was being so effectively fulfilled, that all of Asia Minor, both Jews and Greeks, heard the Gospel of Jesus Christ in just two years.

The power of the Gospel of Jesus Christ has the same impact upon cities and regions, today, when a local church, or community of churches, catches the vision and passion of the Great Commission. George Otis, Jr. has documented the modern day impact of Jesus' command in two videos: "Transformation" and "Transformations II".

---

[1] Matthew 28:18-19
[2] Acts 5:28
[3] Acts 17:6

Making disciples is the most important work of the Church and it is the most effective means for transforming homes, cities and communities. It will raise up prayer warriors and intercessors. Anointed and effective workers will be equipped for the various ministries. The foundation for loyal and dedicated leaders will be established. The torch for advancing the Kingdom of God will be passed on to the next generation!

Making disciples requires much time and it is extremely labor intensive. There is no greater joy and excitement experienced in a family than when a newborn baby is brought home from the hospital. It is the same for the family of God when effective discipleship ministry is taking place. The pastor and the congregation have the privilege of watching newborn babies grow into maturity.

God's heart is passionate about seeing His children grow into Christ-like maturity and become effective ambassadors for His Kingdom. The pastor and local church who will make the choice to give discipleship top priority and quality effort will receive a great reward. The Heavenly Father will be glorified, Jesus Christ will be exalted and the fruit of their labor will remain. (John 15:8-16)

The Holy Spirit birthed a vision in my heart in the late 1970's. God was graciously giving new converts to our ministry and I longed to see them grow and become mighty in Spirit. The resources I found were very few. The majority of the discipleship material that was available did not teach the new believer how to receive the gift of the baptism of the Holy Spirit or how to walk in the power of an anointed life. The Spirit-filled resources on the market lacked depth and balance. I began earnestly seeking the Lord, asking Him to help me write material for the new believers He was giving to our ministry. I longed to see the new believer become mature, filled with the Holy Spirit and effective in "doing the work of the ministry". (Eph. 4:12) I also wanted to train the established believers, so they could become effective in sharing their faith, praying for others and able to train new disciples themselves.

The teaching outlines in this manual are the result of over twenty years of teaching discipleship courses and equipping young believers for Kingdom service. These teachings have literally been covered with hours of intercession and soaked with many tears. My heart has been filled with joy as I have watched those who knew little of the

Scriptures or of Jesus Christ, grow to maturity and become established as strong disciples. I have rejoiced, watching established believers become effective workers who were "able to teach others also" (II Timothy 2:2). Some of those disciples are in full time Christian ministry today and others are effective missionaries in their work place. My prayer is that you will find the great joy and reward I have found in sharing these teachings.

"By this is My Father glorified, that you bear much fruit, and so prove to be My disciples… You did not choose Me, but I chose you, and appointed you, that you should go and bear fruit, and that your fruit should remain, that whatever you ask of the Father in My name, He may give to you. This I command you, that you love one another."[4]

---

[4] John 15:8, 16-17 (NAS)

What is a Disciple

I. **The definition of a disciple**

   A. From Strong's concordance

   Strong's # 3101 "mathetes" (math-ay-tes'); from .3129: a learner, i.e. pupil; KJV "disciple."[5]

   B. From Vine's dictionary of the New Testament:

   1. Noun

   - *mathetes* NT: 3101, lit., "a learner" (from *manthano*, "to learn," from a root math--, indicating thought accompanied by endeavor), in contrast to *didaskalos*, "a teacher"; hence it denotes "one who follows one's teaching," as the "disciples" of John, Matt 9:14; of the Pharisees, Matt 22:16; of Moses, John 9:28; it is used of the "disciples" of Jesus (a) in a wide sense, of Jews who became His adherents, John 6:66; Luke 6:17, some being secretly so, John 19:38; (b) especially of the twelve apostles, Matt 10:1; Luke 22:11, e.g.; (c) of all who manifest that they are His "disciples" by abiding in His Word, John 8:31cf. 13:35; 15:8; (d) in Acts, of those who believed upon Him and confessed Him, 6:1,2,7; 14:20, 22, 28; 15:10; 19:1:

       a) A "disciple" was not only a pupil, but an adherent; hence they are spoken of as imitators of their teacher; cf. John 8:31; 15:8.

       b) "Mathetria" NT: 3102, "a female disciple," - Acts 9:36.

       c) "Summathetes" NT: 4827 means "a fellow disciple" (sun, with, and No. 1), John 11:16.

   Note: In Acts 1:15, the RV translates the manuscripts which have "adelphon", brethren; in 20:7, RV, "we," for KJV, "disciples."

   2. Verb

   - "matheteuo" NT: 3100 is used in the active voice, intransitively, in some manuscripts, in Matthew 27:57, in the sense of being the "disciple" of a person; here, however, the best manuscripts have the passive voice, lit., "had been made a disciple," as in Matt 13:52, RV, "who hath been made a disciple." it is used in this transitive sense in the active voice in Matt. 28:19 and Acts 14:21.[6]

   C. Matthew 10:1-4 - the call of the twelve disciples

---

[5] James Strong, S.T.D., LL.D, "The Exhaustive Concordance of the Bible, Greek Dictionary of the New Testament", (New York and Nashville, 1890), p. 45.

[6] Vine's Expository Dictionary of Biblical Words, Copyright (c)1985, Thomas Nelson Publishers

1. Luke 10:20 - names written in heaven
2. Need to ask what true salvation is and define it.
3. True salvation is to:
   a) acknowledge you are a sinner by admitting to God He is right about your behavior and its consequences;
   b) believe God's provision for salvation in Jesus Christ;
   c) confess your sins to God;
   d) ask His forgiveness;
   e) believe He does forgive;
   f) ask Jesus Christ to come into your heart;
   g) yield to Him as Lord of your life;

D. Matt. 10:24-42 - the place of a disciple - Luke 6:40

E. Mark 9:31/ Mark 10:32-44 - servant of all

F. John 14:21-25 / John 15:12-15 - obeys his master

G. John 13:34-35 - love for one another

H. John 6: 50-69 - hear and receive His hard teachings

I. John 1.9:1r-21 - hated of the world

J. John 15:26, 27 / Matt. 10:32 - bear witness of Jesus

K. John 15:8 - bear much fruit

L. John 17:12-17 – "not of the world"

II. **The cost of discipleship to me as an individual**

A. Matt. 16:24-25 / Mark 8:35 / Luke 9:24 – "lose his life"

B. Matt. 19:16-30 – "forsake all to follow Jesus"

C. John 6:38-66 – a disciple accepts and surrenders to the truth and principles of God's Word no matter what it costs them

D. Matt 7:21 / Matt. 12:50 - surrender your will to the will of your Heavenly Father as Jesus surrendered His will to the Father.

III. **The life goal of a disciple**

A. John 17:4, 18 - do the work that the Father has sent them to do - John 20:21, *"then said Jesus to them again, peace be unto you: as my Father has sent Me, even so I send you."*

B. Matt. 5:5-15 / Luke 10:1-11 - take cities for Jesus

C. Matt. 28:19 - make disciples of all nations

What is a Disciple – Student Handout

I. The definition of a disciple

    A. _____

    B. _____

        1. _____

        2. _____

    C. _____

        1. _____

        2. _____

        3. _____

            a) _____

            b) _____

            c) _____

            d) _____

            e) _____

            f) _____

            g) _____

D. _____

E. _____

F. _____

G. _____

H. _____

I. _____

J. _____

K. _____

L. _____

II. **The cost of discipleship to me as an individual**

A. _____

B. _____

C. _____

D. _____

III. **The life goal of a disciple**

A. _____

B. _____

C. _____

Notes

Discipleship is More Than Excitement...It is Responsibility

Introduction:

You are a supervisor at a local business and you are hiring a new employee. When interviewing personnel for the position, what qualifications would you look for in a person? The apostle Paul addressed this very issue regarding disciples in I Corinthians 4:1-2 and in II Timothy 2:1-5.

- **"Steward"**

  - Strong's: # 3623 – "oikonomos" from 3624 and the base of 3551; a house-distributor (i.e. manager), or overseer, i.e. an employee in that capacity; by extension, a fiscal agent (treasure); figuratively, a preacher (of the Gospel): KJV - chamberlain, governor, steward.[7]

  - Thayer's: - the manager of a household or of household affairs, steward, manager, superintendent, (whether free-born or as was usually the case, a freed-man or slave) to whom the head of the house or proprietor has entrusted the management of his affairs the care of receipts and expenditures, and the duty of dealing out the proper portion to every servant and even to the children not yet of age,... The superintendent of the city's finances, the treasure of the city.[8]

- **"Required"**

  - Strong's: #2212 – "zeto"; of uncertain affinity; to seek (literally or figuratively); specially, (by Hebraism) to worship (God), or (in a bad sense) to plot (against life); KJV – be (go) about, desire, endeavor, enquire (for), require, (X will) seek (after, for, means), compare 4441.[9]

  - Thayer's: - to seek in order to find, to seek (i.e. in order to find out) by thinking, meditating reasoning; to inquire into; require, demand.[10]

- **"Faithful"**

  - Strong's: #4103 – "pistos" from 3982; objectively, trustworthy; subjectively, trustful; KJV - believe (-ing,-), faithful (-ly), sure, true.[11]

  - Thayer's: - trusty, faithful; of persons who show themselves faithful in the transaction of business, the execution of commands, or the discharge of official duties... worth of trust that can be relied upon.[12]

---

[7] James Strong, S.T.D., L.L.D., <u>Exhaustive Concordance of the Bible, Greek Dictionary of the New Testament</u> (New York, Nashville, 1890), p. 51.
[8] Joseph Henry Thayer, D.D., <u>Greek-English Lexicon of the New Testament</u> (Grand Rapids, 1976), pp. 440-441.
[9] Strong's Exhaustive
[10] Thayer's Lexicon
[11] Strong's Exhaustive
[12] Thayer's Lexicon

I. **Jesus' teaching on faithfulness**

   A. Little things - Luke 16:10

      1. "Faithful in little things" deals with the difference between being faithful and being unjust.

      2. Unjust is "one who violates or has violated justice, one who breaks God's laws, unrighteous, sinful, especially of one who deals fraudulently with others."[13]

      3. Jesus equated failure to keeping irresponsibility of even the smallest size as unjust, fraudulent and sinful.

      4. Small responsibilities of the believer are:

         a) reading the Word daily,

         b) praying daily,

         c) church attendance,

         d) forgiving all who offend you;

   B. Use of finances and true riches of the Kingdom - Luke 16:11

      1. KJV uses the word "mammon". It is a word from Aramaic origin meaning wealth, avarice, treasure, riches that are trusted in.

      2. Jesus commanded the followers to be faithful in following His example of the use of finances, for then they would receive the true riches of the Kingdom.

      3. Faithful use of finances are:

         a) tithing (Malachi 3:8-12)

         b) first fruits of labor (Proverbs 3:9-10)

         c) supporting and blessing the man of God - (Philippians 4:15-19)

         d) having a right attitude about giving - (II Corinthians 9:1-7)

      4. When this is joyfully followed true riches will be poured out upon your life.

         a) II Corinthians 9:8-15 - grace will abound through your life unto others

         b) I Peter 4:7-11 – you will be a good steward of God's grace in the lives of others

         c) Matthew 25:14-30 – you will be given responsibility in God's Kingdom

   C. ... You will receive your own place of work and ministry - Luke 16:12

---

[13] Thayer's Lexicon

1. When you are faithful to serve another person you will be given your own.
2. Faithful to serve another is having a servant's heart and a desire to make someone else successful. It is the Old Testament concept of being an armor bearer:
   a) to your parents,
   b) to your employer, manager, supervisor (customers, vendors, etc.),
   c) to your pastor and local church;
3. "Faithful" means dependable, loyal, trustworthy (integrity), do your best every time, you "show up," follow through with even the smallest assignments, you carry a sense of obligation
4. The promise - you will be blessed with receiving your own position, promotion, company, etc. Proverbs 28:20, Luke 19:17, Joseph was promoted each time, David was anointed king from being a faithful shepherd; God will see you and reward you.

II. Important areas to be faithful

A. God's Word

1. II Timothy 2:15
2. Definitions from II Timothy 2:15

   "Study"

   - Strong's: #4704 – "spoudazo" from 4710; to use speed, i.e., to make effort, be prompt or earnest: KJV -- do (give) diligence, be diligent (forward), endeavor, labor, study.[14]
   - Thayer's: - hasten, to make haste, to exert one's self, endeavor, give diligence[15]

   "Approved"

   - Strong's: #1384 – "dokimos" from 1380; properly, acceptable (current after assail), i.e. approved KJV- approved, tried.[16]
   - Thayer's: - accepted, particularly of coins and metals, proved, tried, one who is of tried faith and integrity, acceptable, pleasing.[17]

   "Dividing"

   - Strong's: #3718 – "orthotomeo"; from a compound of 3717 and the base of 5114, to make a straight cut, i.e. (figuratively) to dissect

---

[14] Strong's Exhaustive
[15] Thayer's Lexicon
[16] Strong's Exhaustive
[17] Thayer's Lexicon

- (Expound) correctly (the divine message); KJV-- rightly divide, 5719 "orthrizo"; from 3722; to use the dawn, i.e. (by implication) to repair betimes; KJV- come early in the morning.[18]
- <u>Thayer's</u>: - to cut straight (ways, paths) hold a straight course, to do, to handle aright, to teach the truth correctly and directly.[19]

5. Psalm 119:1-4, 9, 97-105
6. Set a specific time and location for each day and be consistent.
7. Take notes in church and review them weekly, do historical research, word studies, character studies.
8. Get good resources.

B. Daily prayer
1. Ephesians 6:18
2. I Timothy 2:1-4
3. Luke 18:1-18
4. Set a specific time and location daily and study resources on intercessory prayer.

C. Finances
1. Malachi 3:8-10
2. Proverbs 3:9-10
3. II Corinthians 8:1-5
4. II Corinthians 9:1-9

D. Church attendance
1. Acts 2:40-42
2. Hebrews 10:19-25
3. Acts 9:31-32, Acts 19:8-10

---

[18] Strong's Exhaustive
[19] Thayer's Lexicon

Discipleship is More Than Excitement…it is Responsibility – Student Handout

I Corinthians 4:2   II Timothy 2:4-5

"Steward" means:

_____

_____

_____

"Required" means: _____

_____

_____

"Faithful" means: _____

_____

_____

I. Jesus' teaching on faithfulness

    A. Little things - Luke 16:10

        1. _____

        _____

        2. _____

        _____

        3. _____

        _____

        4. _____

B. Use of finances and true riches of the Kingdom - Luke 16:11

    1. _____

       _____

    2. _____

       _____

    3. _____

        a) _____

        b) _____

        c) _____

        d) _____

    4. _____

        a) _____

        b) _____

        c) _____

C. ... Will receive your own place of work and ministry - Luke 16:12

    1. _____

    2. _____

       _____

        a) _____

        b) _____

        c) _____

3. _____
_____

4. _____
_____

II. Important areas to be faithful

A. _____

1. _____

2. _____

"Study"

_____
_____
_____

"Approved"

_____
_____
_____

"Dividing"

_____
_____
_____

3. _____

4. _____

5. _____

6. _____
   _____

B. _____

   1. _____

   2. _____

   3. _____

   4. _____

C. _____

   1. _____

   2. _____

   3. _____

   4. _____

D. _____

   1. _____

   2. _____

   3. _____

Notes

Dealing with Myself and the World - Four Levels of Conflict

Introduction:

The apostle Paul said in II Corinthians 10:3-5:

"For though we live in the world, we do not wage war as the world does. The weapons we fight with are not the weapons of the world. On the contrary, they have divine power to demolish strongholds." (NIV)

It is not difficult to understand why the Apostle uses the analogy of war to describe our life and the conflicts we face in our daily living. There are days we truly feel like we have been in a battle. Whether it is with our coworkers, our boss, our mate, our children or the other people on the freeway during our commute, we face conflicts.

However, the biggest battle we face is with ourselves - daily fighting inner conflicts with our mind, our emotions, our will, addictions, temptations, appetites. There are many kinds of conflicts we face within ourselves that must be won. It is important to understand that there are four levels to these conflicts we fight - if lasting victory is to be won. Each level of conflict carries a greater measure of struggle, but also brings greater measures of lasting reward, when the battles are won.

Let's look at these four levels of conflict and how they are structured within our life. We will also learn how we can conquer these areas of conflict with the blood of Jesus Christ, the truth of God's word and the power of the Holy Spirit.

I. **Four levels of conflict in every person's life**

   A. The symptoms

   1. Addictions to smoking, alcohol, prescription drugs, illegal drugs, gambling
   2. Eating disorders, chronic sickness, pornography, lying, stealing, cheating, cursing
   3. Poor hygiene, laziness, revealing dress, under achievement, argumentative, temper
   4. All of these are in the area of the flesh and are symptoms of deeper problems in the area of the soul.

   B. Conflicts of the soul

   1. Fear, worry, anxiety, jealousy, frustration, insecurity,
   2. Rejection, low self-acceptance, inferiority, envy, guilt, rebellion, anger, stubbornness
   3. All of these are in the area of the soul and involve negative areas of the mind, emotions and will.

4. It is at this level that almost all counseling, psychology, psychiatry and twelve step programs try to help. This is like dealing with dandelions by mowing the lawn.

C. Three core conflicts - I John 2:15-17

1. Notice there are three areas of conflict known to all mankind
2. Lust of the flesh – immorality:
    a) fornication is premarital sex;
    b) adultery is extramarital sex;
    c) perversion is unnatural sex, using the body in a way for which it was not designed;
3. Lust of the eyes – greed:
    a) Placing my worth in wealth or possessions. "I feel like I have greater status, worth or value because I own…"
    b) Placing my security in wealth or possessions. "I feel more secure because I have..."
4. Pride of life - iniquity - self-willed living
    a) Self-willed living is having the final word over a matter or over my life;
    b) Self-willed living is holding unforgiveness, bitterness, and hatred toward a person who has hurt or wronged you;
    c) That person may have gone to the Father and received salvation and forgiveness of their sin; yet you hold it against them when God has granted them forgiveness - you place yourself above God.
5. These three areas deal with conflicts within the spirit of man.
6. They manifest themselves in the flesh and in the soul but they are spiritual issues and the resolution is found in the spirit.

D. The solution to all conflict - Hebrews 12:14-17

1. The source of all conflict within the heart of man is found in this passage.
2. Cain is the biblical example of mankind's conflict.
3. He resisted the grace of God, became bitter, immoral and greedy.
4. What is grace? "Grace is the desire to do God's will and the strength to carry it out."[20]
5. If grace is resisted a root of bitterness is implanted and it will defile "many." (Greek – *"polus"* - much, large)[21]

---

[20] Bill Gothard, speaking at the Institute in Basic Life Principles, Seattle 1981

6. When an individual chooses to resist God's grace a large portion of their life and of their relationships are damaged by setting off all the areas of conflict.

E. The apostle Paul's amazing discovery - II Corinthians 12:7-10

1. He had a "buffeter from Satan" and asked God three times to remove it.
2. God's answer was, "My grace is sufficient."
3. Paul actually found "delight" in the conflict, how can that be possible?
4. God's strength was made perfect (complete) in the areas of Paul's weakness. How is that possible?
5. Through God's grace, Paul was given the desire and the ability to do God's will in each circumstance.
6. The same promise is given to every believer in Romans 5:21.

II. God's wonderful solution to conflict

A. God's "iron clad" promise

1. I Corinthians 10:13
2. You are not exclusive
3. God can be trusted, He is faithful
4. He has set a "load limit" on your life
5. He will provide a way of victory that you may be able to bear it.
6. His way of escape is His grace that is sufficient.

B. When we resist we face great danger

1. Ephesians 4:26-32
2. When we resist God's grace we give an area of "jurisdiction" to the devil.
3. The powers of darkness use that area to establish a stronghold.
4. Matthew 18:32-34 - we are then turned over to the tormentor and many areas of conflict arise within our soul and flesh.

III. Steps to amazing victory and conquering all levels of conflict within our soul and flesh

A. God's grace is eternal

1. God's love offers us compassion and mercy. His mercy offers us grace to be saved and to live victoriously on a daily basis.
2. Because God's mercy is everlasting, His grace is eternally offered making available to us the grace that was offered but resisted in past years.

---

[21] Joseph Henry Thayer, D.D., Greek-English Lexicon of the New Testament, (Grand Rapids 1976) p. 529

3. You can open your heart today to the grace that was offered and receive the same desire and ability to do God's will now even in areas of past failures.

4. All you must do is be willing to open your heart and accept God's grace.

B. Release judgment and accountability against the offender

1. Make a list of all who have offended you and of their hurts and offenses.

2. Repent and ask God's forgiveness for resisting His grace in the past.

3. Open your heart and receive His grace now and extend forgiveness.

4. Release all judgment against the offender.

5. Release all accountability against the offender.

6. Burn the list as a sign of letting all of the offenses go.

C. Ask for God's heart and eyes for the offender

1. Offer to God your heart and allow Him to love the person through you.

2. Offer to God your eyes so you can look at the offender with God's eyes of mercy and compassion.

3. Choose to pray blessings on the offender every day.

4. Continue to do this daily.

Dealing with Myself and the World – Four Levels of Conflict – Student Handout

I. Four levels of conflict in every person's life

    A. The symptoms

    _____

    _____

    _____

    B. Conflicts of the soul

    _____

    _____

    _____

    C. Three core conflicts – I John 2:15-17

        1. _____

        2. _____

            a) _____

            b) _____

            c) _____

        3. _____

a) _____

b) _____

4. _____

a) _____

b) _____

c) _____

5. _____

6. _____

D. The solution to all conflict – Hebrews 12:14-17

E. The apostle Paul's amazing discovery – II Corinthians 12:7-10

_____

_____

_____

_____

_____

_____

II. God's wonderful solution

    A. God's _____ - I Corinthians 10:13

_____

_____

_____

_____

_____

    B. When we resist we _____

        1. Ephesians 4:26-32

        2. _____

3. _____

4. Matthew 18:32-34

   _____
   _____
   _____

III. **Steps to amazing victory and conquering all levels of conflict within our soul and flesh**

   A. _____

   1. _____
   _____

   2. _____
   _____

   3. _____
   _____

   4. _____

   B. _____

   1. _____

   2. _____

   3. _____

   4. _____

   5. _____

6. _____

C. _____

1. _____

2. _____

3. _____

4. _____

Notes

My Body...an Instrument of Righteousness

I. Romans 12:1-2

    A. What are we supposed to do with our bodies?

       - Present them as a living sacrifice

       - What does that mean? (Ask and get response)

    B. Why are we supposed to do this?

       - As an act of worship (v. 1)

       - To Show God's will in our lives (v.2)

    C. What happens when we follow through?

       - transform our behavior patterns by renewing our mind

       - conform our life to the image of Jesus Christ

II. How does all this happen? - Romans 6:1-14

    A. The first principle

        Sin shall not have dominion over you (v. 14)

        Reference to the sin nature not sins (deeds)

        We do not live under the lordship (mastery) of sin

        Grace has broke that power

          - 1 John 3:5-10 (Amp.)

          - Hebrews 9:1-15

          - II Cor. 5:17 / Titus 3:4-5 / Rom. 8:11-12

    B. The second principle

       1. Identify yourself as "alive to God and dead to sin" (v. 11)

       2. Compare Romans 6:11 with II Corinthians 5:19 *reckon* and *imputing* (in KJV) are the same word in Greek

       3. We are to identify with the finished work of Jesus

       4. See yourself (crucified, buried, risen with Jesus)

    C. The third principle

       1. Do not let sin reign (v.12)

2. This is dealing with the authority of darkness in your life and behavior

3. Look at Col. 1:13

4. This is dealing with stronghold of darkness and taking back the territory given over to his authority II Cor. 10:3-5

D. The fourth principle

1. Yield the members of your body to righteousness

2. This deals with how we use the individual members of our body to do right or to participate in the sinful

3. It is a choice of our will

4. We must deal rightly with temptation (we will discuss this issue in a few weeks)

My Body...An Instrument of Righteousness – Student Handout

I.   Romans 12:1-2

  A. What are we supposed to do with our bodies?

  - _____

  - _____

  B. Why are we supposed to do this?

  - _____

  - _____

  C. What happens when we follow through?

  - _____

  - _____

II.   How does all this happen? - Romans 6:1-14

  A. The first principle

   1. _____

   2. _____

   3. _____

   4. _____

B. The second principle

    1. _____

       _____

    2. _____

    3. _____

C. The third principle

    1. _____

    2. _____

    3. _____

    4. _____

       _____

D. The fourth principle

    1. _____

    2. _____

    3. _____

    4. _____

Notes

Becoming Like Jesus by Rebuilding My Thought Patterns and Transforming My Thinking

Introduction:

Read the following Scriptures with the students:

- Isaiah 55:8-9
- Romans 1:21
- Philippians 2:5
- Romans 12:2
- Ephesians 4:22-24
- James 1:21
- Proverbs 23:7

I.   The problem the believer faces with "stinkin' thinkin'"

A. We are born and raised with it

1. The great battle faced by all believers, when seeking to become like Jesus, is fought in our mind.

2. The thinking of the natural man is upside down to God and in direct opposition to His Word.

3. Thought patterns are established from our earliest days through family training and are shaped by years of education.

4. A person's thought patterns shape their behavior and impact their relationship with God.

B. Look at three very poignant examples in Scripture.

1. Genesis 6:5-6 (NKJ)

"...Then the Lord saw that the wickedness of man was great in the earth, and that every intent of the thoughts of his heart was only evil continually. And the Lord was sorry that He had made man on the earth, and He was grieved in His heart."

The wickedness of their thought patterns shaped their lives and culture with such corruption that God had to send judgment.

2. Romans 1:21-22 (KJV)

"...Because that, when they knew God, they glorified Him not as God, neither were thankful; but became vain in their imaginations, and their foolish heart was darkened. Professing themselves to be wise, they became fools."

The arrogance of mankind's thinking causes him to accept a humanistic philosophy over God's revelation of Himself, resulting in a heart filled with darkness and a corrupt imagination.

3. Ephesians 4:17-24 (NAS)

"...This I say therefore, and affirm together with the Lord, that you walk no longer just as the gentiles also walk, in the futility of their mind, being darkened in their understanding, excluded from the life of God, because of the ignorance that is in them, because of the hardness of their heart and they, having become callous, have given themselves over to sensuality, for the practice of every kind of impurity with greediness. But you did not learn Christ in this way, if indeed you have heard Him and have been taught in Him, just as truth is in Jesus, that, in reference to your former manner of life, you lay aside the old self, which is being corrupted in accordance with the lusts of deceit, and that you be renewed in the spirit of your mind, and put on the new self, which in {the likeness of} God has been created in righteousness and holiness of the truth."

Paul's reference to *"gentiles"* is not merely speaking of non-Jews. Rather, the apostle is referring to all individuals who have not accepted the salvation through faith in Jesus Christ. Their hearts are hardened through wrong thought patterns; they are driven by passions, immorality and greed.

4. When a person comes to saving faith, Jesus Christ in His purity fills their heart. But, they still have "stinkin' thinkin'"! If a purposeful and diligent effort is not made to change the thought patterns guiding their thinking, they will never experience the victorious and holy life of Jesus Christ.

II. **What are the steps to rebuilding thought patterns?**

A. Romans 12:2 - *"...be ye transformed by the renewing of the mind..."*

1. *Mind* refers to all conscious and subconscious workings of the brain. Included are the intellect, memories, and opinions, thought patterns, value systems, reasoning, ideology, and philosophies.

2. Renewing means to rebuild, renovate, restore something to a sound condition. In this case, it is referencing the restoration of a person's mind to the condition God originally intended, so it is in agreement with God's Word and God's thoughts.

3. The process of renewing a building is a great analogy to the renewing of one's mind - the necessity of removing all wall boarding, siding, replacing all framework that is damaged, lifting the building to repair the foundation, replacing or up-grading all electrical and plumbing.

4. God wants to completely renovate our conscious and subconscious mind with the precepts, principles, and truths of His Word.

B. Fill your mind with the Word of God

1. Take large blocks of Scripture and memorize them for the purpose of learning the truths in their context and for meditation.
2. Memorizing the Word provides the building material the Holy Spirit uses to renovate your mind.
3. Choose an accountability partner for memorizing and practicing quotation.
4. Suggested Scriptures are:
   - James 1 - dealing with temptation
   - Matthew 5-7 - living life by a new world view
   - Hebrews 11 - building faith
   - John 15 - spiritual growth
   - Romans 6-8 - victorious Christian living
   - I Corinthians 13 - God-kind-of-love

C. Saturating your mind with the Word of God
   1. Meditation serves the same purpose as grafting does for a fruit tree.
   2. The old trunk of the tree is able to bring forth a new kind of fruit.
   3. Meditation saturates the conscious and subconscious portion of your brain with the Word of God in its complete context.
   4. This deep implantation provides the ability to transform thought patterns.

III. **What are the steps to transforming thought patterns?**

A. Philippians 4:8
   1. Thoughts are not sin.
   2. Thoughts are the seed sent from the enemy to become the germination of sin.
   3. You cannot stop thoughts from entering.
   4. You can prevent them from being planted and bringing forth their fruit.
   5. It is a decision of your will and a learned spiritual discipline.
   6. It requires purposeful and diligent spiritual work.

B. Expose every thought to God's Word
   1. Discuss wrong thoughts with God - every wrong thought, every time!
   2. Do not hide them or keep them secret - this is the seed bed for the germination of sin

3. Expose the wrong thought to the truths, principles and precepts of the Word.

4. Be specific and quote the Scriptures chosen - even out loud.

C. Express your response by the Word of God

1. Claim specific promises from the Word of God

2. Make the wrong thought subject to that promise

3. Express your response to the wrong thought by the Word of God

4. Fill your mind with the truth and promises of God's Word.

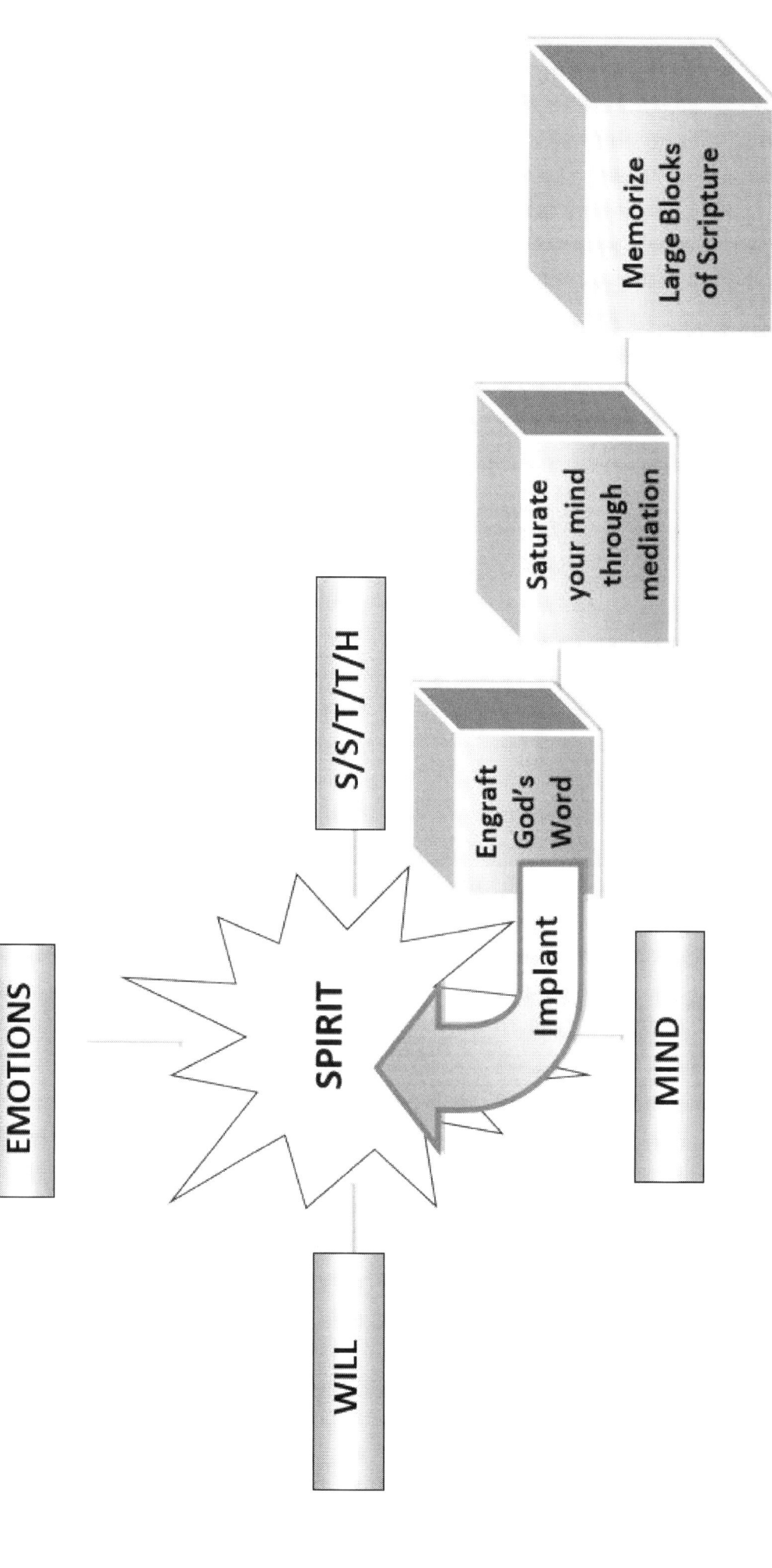

REBUILDING THE PATTERNS OF YOUR MIND

- Engraft God's Word
- Saturate your mind through mediation
- Memorize Large Blocks of Scripture

S/S/T/T/H

Implant

SPIRIT

EMOTIONS

MIND

WILL

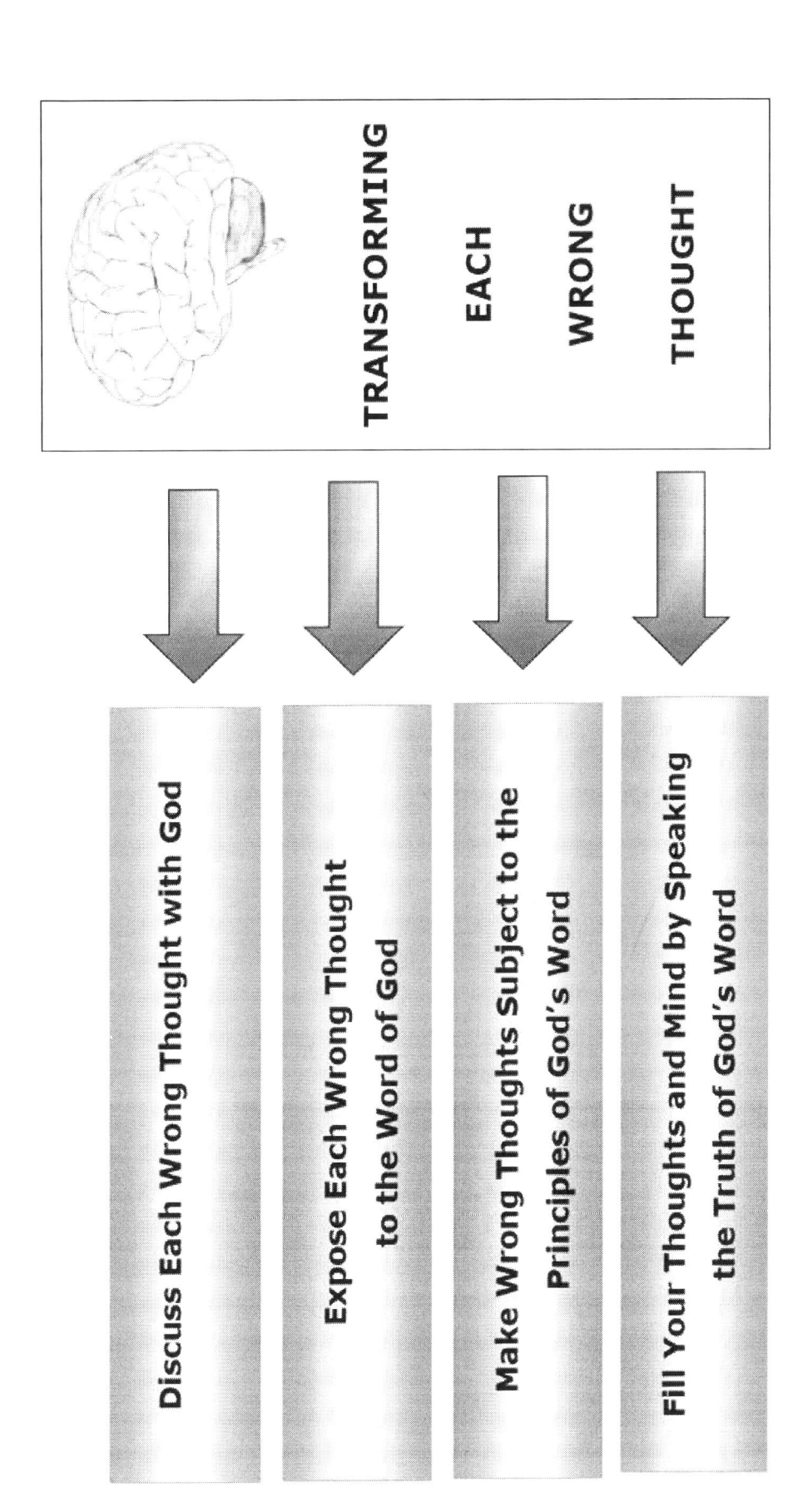

TRANSFORMING EACH WRONG THOUGHT

- Discuss Each Wrong Thought with God
- Expose Each Wrong Thought to the Word of God
- Make Wrong Thoughts Subject to the Principles of God's Word
- Fill Your Thoughts and Mind by Speaking the Truth of God's Word

Becoming Like Jesus by Rebuilding My Thought Patterns and Transforming My Thinking – Student Handout

Read the following Scriptures:

- Isaiah 55:8-9
- Romans 1:21
- Philippians 2:5
- Romans 12:2
- Ephesians 4:22-24
- James 1:21
- Proverbs 23:7

I.   The problem the believer faces with "stinkin' thinkin'"

A. We are born and raised with it

_____

_____

_____

_____

_____

_____

_____

_____

_____

B. Look at three very poignant examples in Scripture.

    1. Genesis 6:5-6 (NKJ)

"... then the Lord saw that the wickedness of man was great in the earth, and that every intent of the thoughts of his heart was only evil continually. And the Lord was sorry that He had made man on the earth, and He was grieved in His heart.

_____

_____

    2. Romans 1:21-22 (KJV)

"... because that, when they knew God, they glorified Him not as God, neither were thankful; but became vain in their imaginations, and their foolish heart was darkened. Professing themselves to be wise, they became fools.

_____

_____

    3. Ephesians 4:17-24 (NAS)

"... this I say therefore, and affirm together with the Lord, that you walk no longer just as the gentiles also walk, in the futility of their mind, being darkened in their understanding, excluded from the life of God, because of the ignorance that is in them, because of the hardness of their heart and they, having become callous, have given themselves over to sensuality, for the practice of every kind of impurity with greediness. But you did not learn Christ in this way, if

indeed you have heard Him and have been taught in Him, just as truth is in Jesus, that, in reference to your former manner of life, you lay aside the old self, which is being corrupted in accordance with the lusts of deceit, and that you be renewed in the spirit of your mind, and put on the new self, which in {the likeness of} God has been created in righteousness and holiness of the truth.

II. What are the steps to rebuilding thought patterns?

A. Romans 12:2- *"be ye transformed by the renewing of the mind..."*

1. _____

2. _____

3. _____

4. _____

5.

B. Fill your mind with the Word of God

1. _____

2. _____

3. _____

   4. Suggested Scriptures are:

      - James 1 - dealing with temptation
      - Matthew 5-7 - living life by a new world view
      - Hebrews 11 - building faith
      - John 15 - spiritual growth
      - Romans 6-8 - victorious Christian living
      - I Corinthians 13 - God-kind-of-love

   C. Saturating your mind with the Word of God

      1. _____

      2. _____

      3. _____

      4. _____

III. What are the steps to transforming thought patterns?

   A. Philippians 4:8

      1. _____

      2. _____

      3. _____

4. _____

5. _____

B. Expose every thought to God's Word

1. _____

2. _____

3. _____

4. _____

C. Express your response by the Word of God

1. _____

2. _____

3. _____

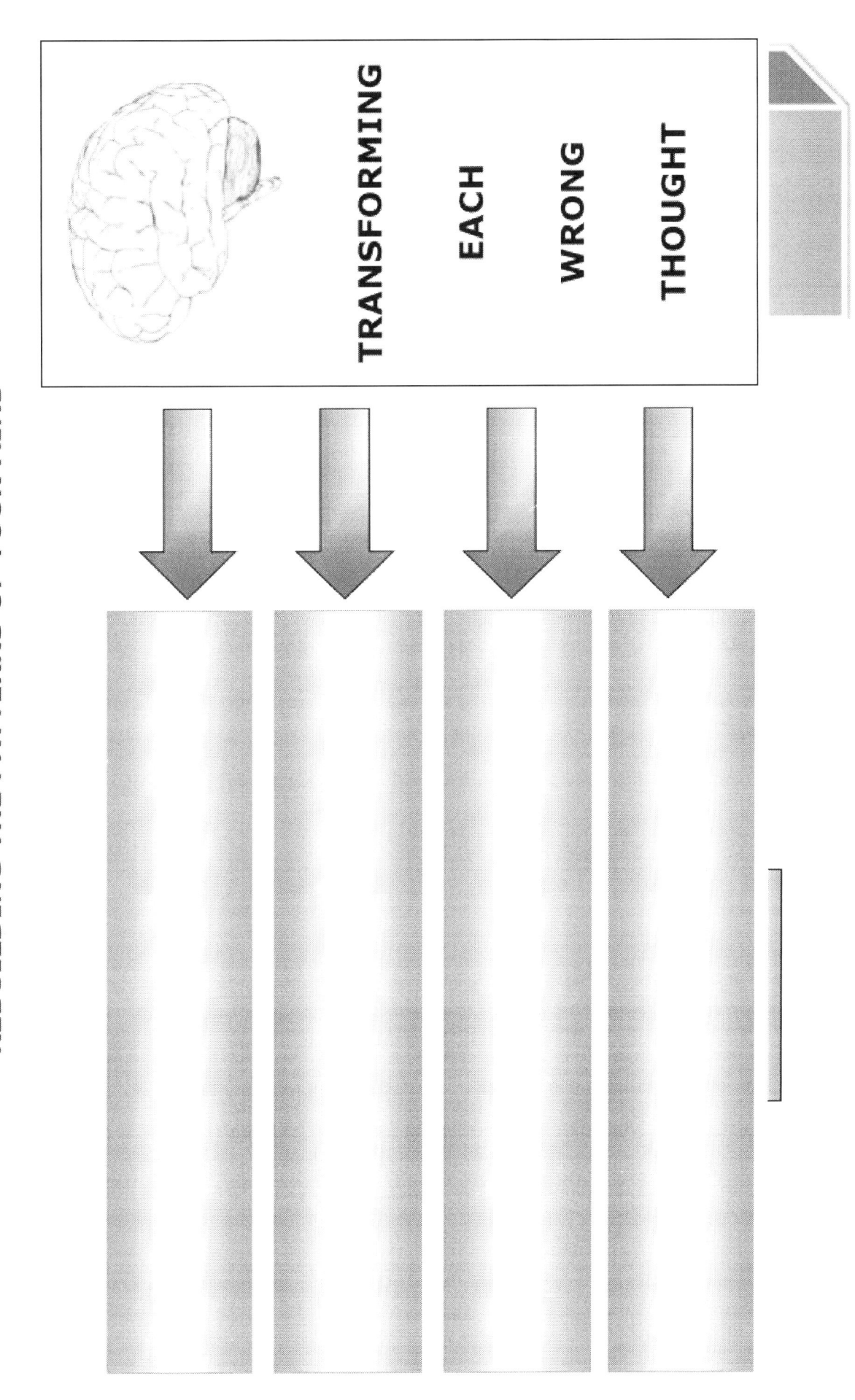

REBUILDING THE PATTERNS OF YOUR MIND

TRANSFORMING EACH WRONG THOUGHT

Notes

Refocusing the Emotions and Redirecting the Will

Introduction

Proverbs 4:18-27

- Our life is to be lived in an ever growing measure of the light of Jesus Christ (I John 1:1-7)

- The unbeliever lives in darkness and does not understand why they stumble.

- If we are to walk in an ever increasing measure of light we must plant the Word of God deep in our heart and let it be the rule of our daily life.

- If we are to walk in light, we must guard our heart with all diligence, for out of it flow the stuff of our life.

- If we are to walk in light we must guard out tongue. Jesus said, "… out of the abundance of the heart the mouth speaks."

- If we are to walk in light we must guard what our eyes view (Matt. 5:27-30).

- If we are to walk in light we must guard where our feet take us.

James gives us the instructions for making this possible (James 1:19-21). He said if we engraft the Word of God into our heart it will save our soul. How does that engrafting take place? Human beings are tri-part creatures - made in the image of God

- Body - made with five senses - sight, smell, taste, touch, hearing (relationship with the created world around)

- Soul - made up of mind, will and emotions (relationship with other human beings)

- Spirit - made with conscience, intuition (God consciousness) and five spiritual senses (relationship with God)

The spirit of man is born again through repentance and the new birth of the Holy Spirit. The soul is saved through the engrafting of the Word of God into our minds through memorizing and meditation. The emotions can then be refocused through the fruit of the Spirit and the will can be redirected to obey God and His Word. Then the appetites and passions of the flesh can be disciplined so the members of the body can become instruments for righteousness (Romans 6:12-14).

I. **The Holy Spirit can renew the mind by rebuilding the thought patterns. Thought patterns are rebuilt by:**

   A. Reading the Bible daily.

   B. Memorizing large portions of Scripture.

   C. Meditating on the passages of Scripture you memorize; early in the morning, throughout the day and night.

II. **Transform wrong thoughts into positive healthy thoughts by:**

   A. Discussing each negative or wrong thought with God through identifying its true nature and consequence.

B. Exposing each negative or wrong thought to the truth of God's Word.

C. Replacing each negative or wrong thought with a truthful statement from Scripture.

D. Expressing your response to each negative or wrong thought through a truthful and positive statement.

III. **The Holy Spirit can refocus your negative or destructive emotions by:**

A. Understanding you cannot trust emotions because they are very subjective and transitory.

B. Exposing negative or destructive emotions to the principles and truthful statements you have been meditating on each day.

C. Expressing your emotions with the truths you are learning through memorization and meditation on God's Word.

D. Replacing the negative and destructive emotions with new ones based upon the truths and principles of God's Word.

IV. **The Holy Spirit can redirect your will (volition) by:**

A. Accepting personal responsibility for being a living translation of the truths and principles of God's Word that you learn

B. Accepting personal responsibility for being a giver not a taker in the community around you.

C. Accepting personal responsibility for exposing each wrong motive and wrong attitude to the principles and truths of God's Word and bringing them to obedience.

D. Accepting personal responsibility for shaping your life, attitude and behavior to conformity of the truth of God's Word.

REFOCUSING THE EMOTIONS

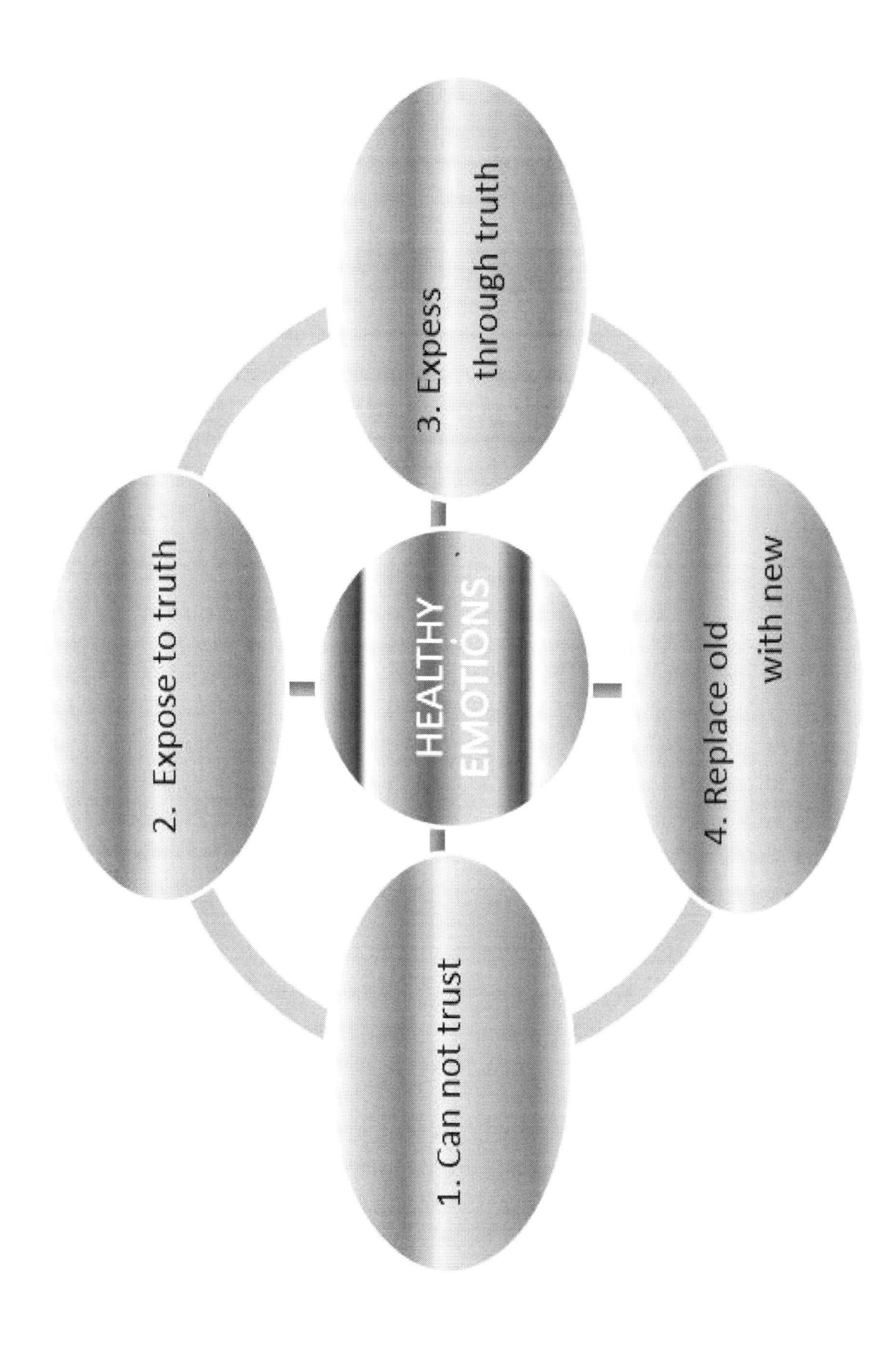

- **HEALTHY EMOTIONS**
- 1. Can not trust
- 2. Expose to truth
- 3. Expess through truth
- 4. Replace old with new

REDIRECTING THE WILL

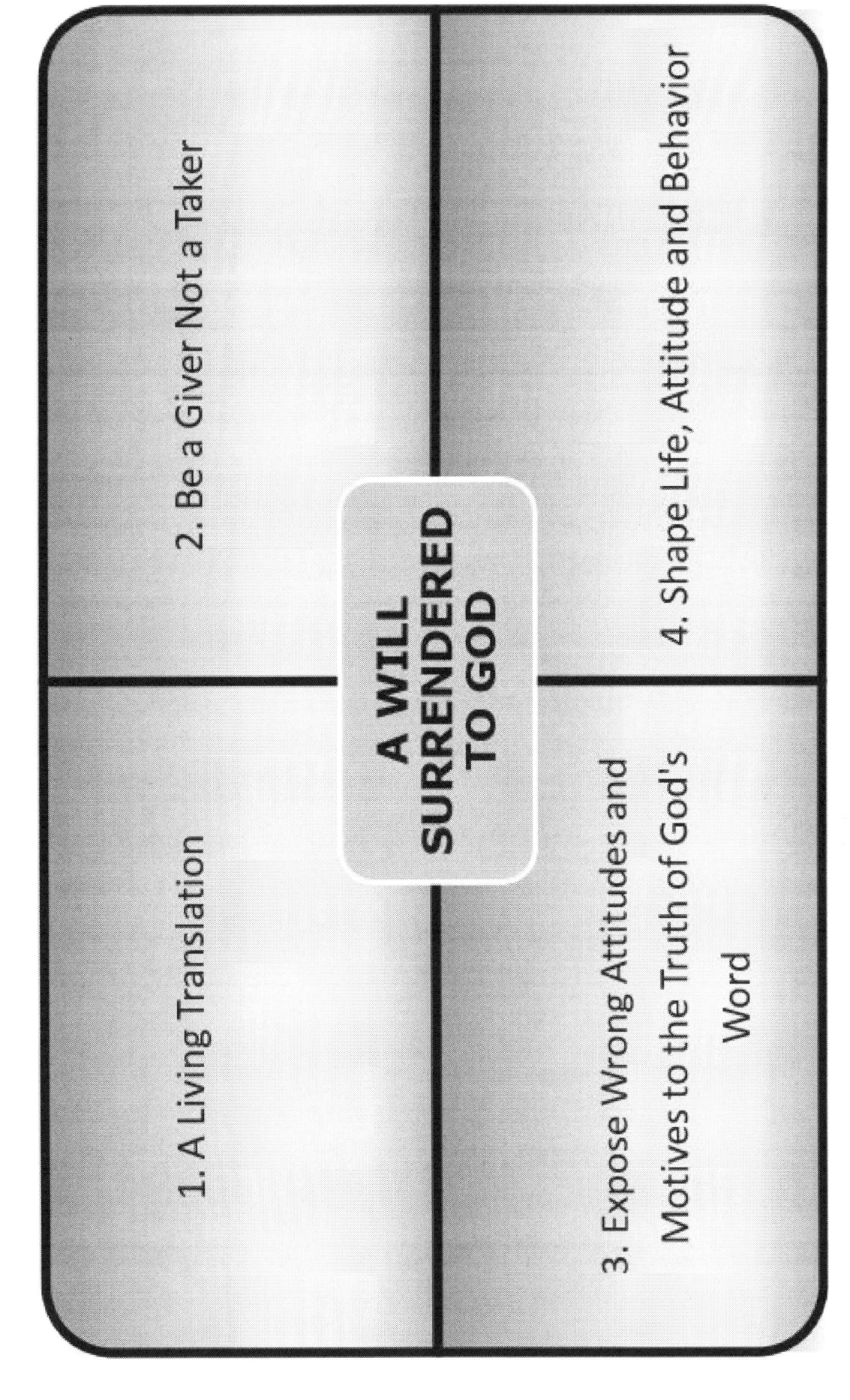

A WILL SURRENDERED TO GOD

1. A Living Translation

2. Be a Giver Not a Taker

3. Expose Wrong Attitudes and Motives to the Truth of God's Word

4. Shape Life, Attitude and Behavior

Refocusing the Emotions and Redirecting the Will – Student Handout

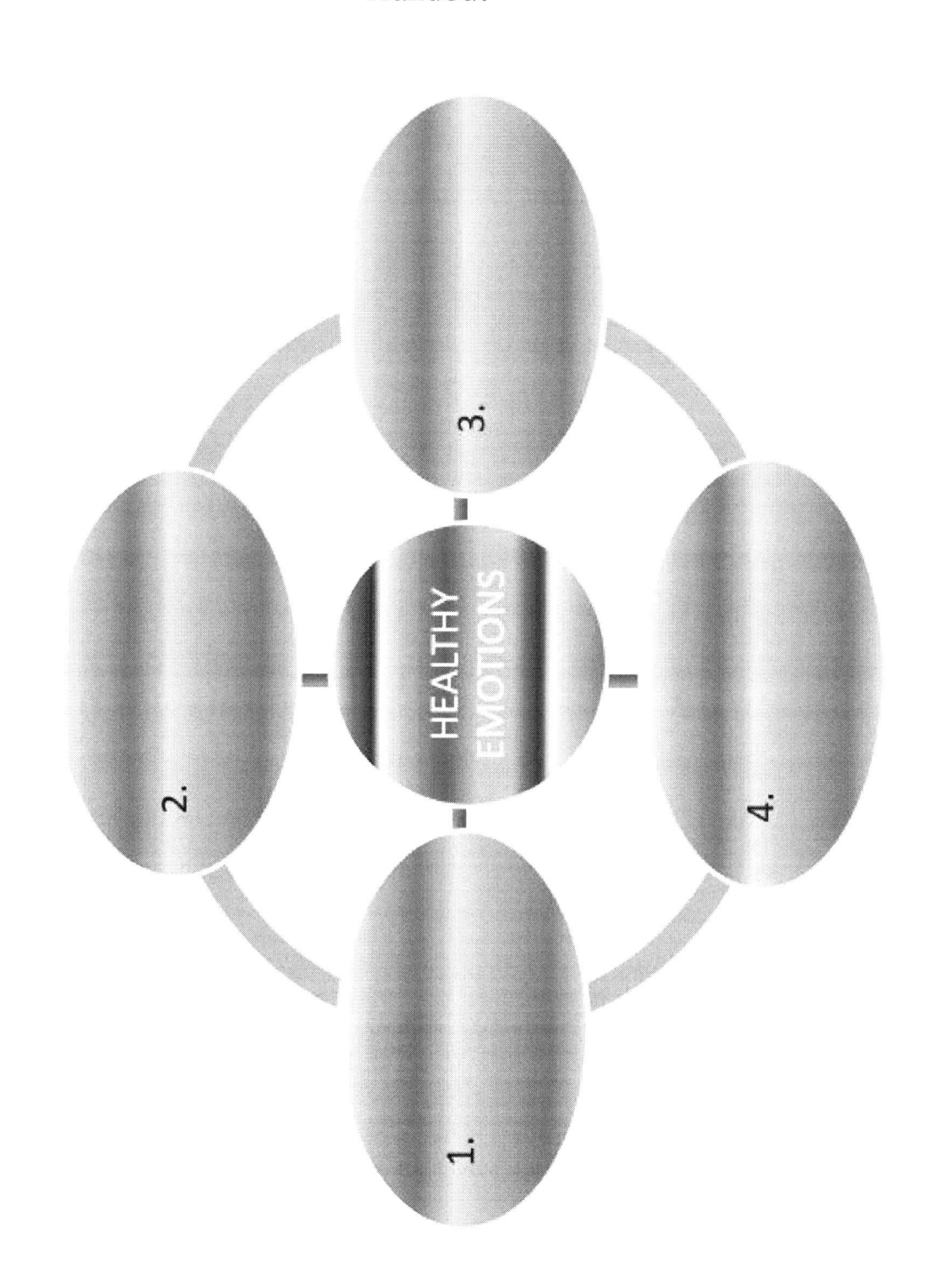

REFOCUSING THE EMOTIONS

HEALTHY EMOTIONS

1.

2.

3.

4.

REDIRECTING THE WILL

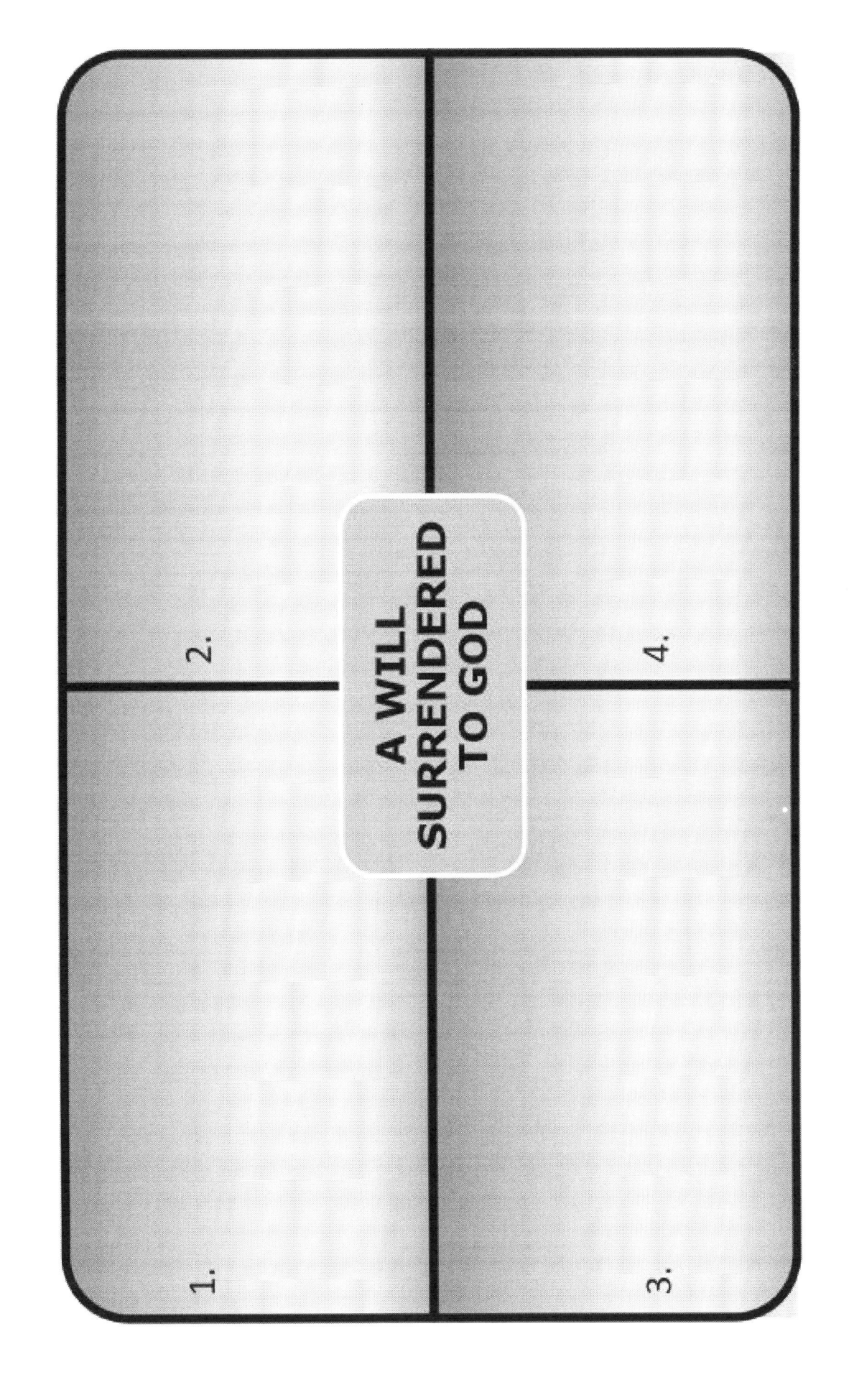

A WILL SURRENDERED TO GOD

1.

2.

3.

4.

Notes

The Secret of True Success in Life...Christian Meditation

I. **What are the promised rewards for the Christian discipline of meditation?**

   A. Joshua 1:8 - will have good success

   B. Psalms 1:2-3 - will experience prosperity in all he does

   C. Psalms 119:97-98 - will be wiser than your enemies

   D. Psalms 119:99-100 - will be wiser than your teachers

   E. Psalms 63:5-6 - will live a life filled with joy

   F. I Timothy 4:15 - your success and prosperity will be visible to all

II. **What is Christian meditation?**

   A. Definition

   OT: 1897 *"Hagah"* -- to moan, to growl, to utter, to muse, to mutter, to meditate, to devise, to plot, to speak

   1. (*Qal*)

      a) to roar, to growl, to groan

      b) to utter, to speak

      c) to meditate, to devise, to muse, to imagine

   2. (*Poal*) - to utter

   3. (*Hiphil*) - to mutter[22]

   OT: 7881 *"siychah"* -- meditation, reflection, a prayer, devotion, a complaint, musing

   1. A complaint

   2. Musing, study (of an object)

   B. How is Christian meditation different from Transcendental Meditation (T.M.)?

   1. T.M. teaches to empty the mind and be passive of heart so as to welcome the influence and evil possession of the demonic.

   2. Christian meditation is the exact opposite.

   3. Christians are not to be passive but are to aggressively seek the Lord.

   4. Christians are not to empty their minds and emotions. They are to fill them with the thoughts and musings of the Word of God so the Holy Spirit can fill.

---

[22] The Online Bible Thayer's Greek Lexicon and Brown Driver & Briggs Hebrew Lexicon, Copyright 1993, Woodside Bible Fellowship, Ontario, Canada. Licensed from the Institute for Creation research

C. Meditation is "rumination" on God's Word
   1. It is memorizing large blocks of Scripture.
   2. It is turning it over and over in your mind and spirit, so it fills your emotions and turns your will.
   3. It is literally chewing on the Word of God all day long.
   4. It requires discipline and diligence.

III. **What analogy does God use in Scripture for the believer?**

   A. Isaiah 53:6 - we are sheep who have gone astray and turned to our own ways. As a result God laid on Jesus Christ all of our iniquity.

   B. John 21:15-19 – *"Peter do you love Me more than these? Then feed My sheep."* We must love God more than any other thing and be willing to feed on His Word for our spiritual food.

   C. Acts 20:28 - the leaders are the shepherds to the flock. They are to watch for our souls.

   D. John 10:11-13 - the Good Shepherd lays down His life for the sheep. We are the sheep and our shepherds are the pastors.

IV. **What are the characteristics for successful meditation on God's Word?**

   A. We must memorize large blocks of Scripture as the source to "chew" on and feed our soul. Sheep always feed then sit down to digest their food in comfortable surroundings.

   B. We must chew our food well and several times to receive full nourishment and maximum benefit of our spiritual food.

   C. We must be accountable if we are going to gain maximum benefit and follow through with the requirement. Sheep need shepherds and so do adults. We must have an accountability partner if we want to succeed.

   D. We must exercise after we have eaten the food. Exercise brings maximum benefit.

The Secret of True Success in Life...Christian Meditation – Student Handout

I. What are the promised rewards for the Christian discipline of meditation?

G. Joshua 1:8 - _____

H. Psalms 1:2-3 - _____

I. Psalms 119:97-98 - _____

J. Psalms 119:99-100 - _____

K. Psalms 63:5-6 - _____

L. I Timothy 4:15 - _____

II. What is Christian meditation?

B. Definition

OT: 1897 *"Hagah"* -- to moan, to growl, to utter, to muse, to mutter, to meditate, to devise, to plot, to speak

    1. (*Qal*)

        d) to roar, to growl, to groan

        e) to utter, to speak

        f) to meditate, to devise, to muse, to imagine

    2. (*Poal*) - to utter

    3. (*Hiphil*) - to mutter[23]

OT: 7881 *"siychah"* -- meditation, reflection, a prayer, devotion, a complaint, musing

---

[23] The Online Bible Thayer's Greek Lexicon and Brown Driver & Briggs Hebrew Lexicon, Copyright 1993, Woodside Bible Fellowship, Ontario, Canada. Licensed from the Institute for Creation research

           1. A complaint
           2. Musing, study (of an object)
    B. How is Christian meditation different from Transcendental Meditation (T.M.)?
           1. T.M. teaches to empty the mind and be passive of heart so as to welcome the influence and evil possession of the demonic.
           2. Christian meditation is the exact opposite.
           3. Christians are not to be passive but are to aggressively seek the Lord.
           4. Christians are not to empty their minds and emotions. They are to fill them with the thoughts and musings of the Word of God so the Holy Spirit can fill.
    C. Meditation is "rumination" on God's Word
           1. It is memorizing large blocks of Scripture.
           2. It is turning it over and over in your mind and spirit, so it fills your emotions and turns your will.
           3. It is literally chewing on the Word of God all day long.
           4. It requires discipline and diligence.

III. **What analogy does God use in Scripture for the believer?**

   E. Isaiah 53:6 - we are _____ who have _____
   _____

   F. John 21:15-19 – *"Peter, do you _____?*
   *Then*_____
   _____

   G. Acts 20:28 - the leaders are _____ to the
   _____

   H. John 10:11-13 - the Good Shepherd
   _____ for _____

IV. **What are the characteristics for successful meditation on God's Word?**

- 62 -

E. _____

F. _____

G. _____

H. _____

Notes

Dealing with Temptation

James 1:12-16

I. **Three points about sin you need to remember**

   A. All believers are tempted

   B. Temptation is a stepping stone to victory

   C. God does not tempt us with evil

II. **The anatomy of temptation**

   A. How does temptation happen?

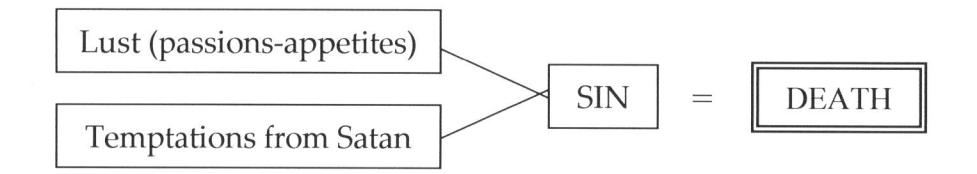

   ```
   [Lust (passions-appetites)] ┐
                                ├──> [SIN] = [DEATH]
   [Temptations from Satan]    ┘
   ```

   B. What is the trick Satan uses?

   1. He sends thoughts into your mind
   2. He makes you think they are yours
   3. He uses deception to make it look good and appealing
   4. Thoughts are not the same as sin unless you dwell on them
   5. You must cut them off before they begin to dwell in your mind

III. **How do you cut off temptation before it becomes sin?**

   A. Love for God and love from God

   1. Sin builds walls in relationships - love cuts off those things that break relationships
   2. Love causes you to turn from the things that would hinder, wound and damage the person you love
   3. Cultivate love for God and love for the things of God
   4. Build your love life for God

B. Uncover the deception of sin
   1. Learn the true consequences of sin
   2. Read a Proverb a day to develop this concept in your life
   3. Build thoughts and emotions and a will that agree with God's statements, laws and ways about sin
   4. Proclaim the truth of God's Word at every temptation
C. Establish a prayer focus:
   1. Pray for a person who needs salvation that would do serious damage to Satan's kingdom
   2. Pray for the person who tempts - picture, neighbor, coworker, star
D. Pray in tongues consistently
   1. Develop the habit of praying in tongues daily - throughout the day

Dealing with Temptation – Student Handout

James 1:12-16

I.   Three points about sin you need to remember

   A. _____

   B. _____

   C. _____

II.   The anatomy of temptation

   B. How does temptation happen?

   ┌─────────────┐
   │   │╲
   └─────────────┘ ╲   ┌─────┐   ┌─────┐
                    ─│   │ = │   │
   ┌─────────────┐ ╱   └─────┘   └─────┘
   │   │╱
   └─────────────┘

   B. What is the trick Satan uses?

   1. _____

   2. _____

   3. _____

   4. _____

   5. _____

III. How do you cut off temptation before it becomes sin?

A. _____

_____

_____

B. _____

_____

_____

C. _____

_____

_____

D. _____

_____

_____

Notes

A Disciple's Love Life

Introduction:

Read the following Scriptures in class

- Matthew 22:36-40
- John 13:34 / John 15:9-10
- I John 2:5 / I John 2:9-11 / I John 2:15-16 / I John 3:10-11 / I John 3:14-19
- I John 3:23 / I John 4:7-21

I.   What are the four Greek words for love?

   A. *"Eros"*
   1. Erotic
   2. Sensuous
   3. "An over-mastering passion seizing upon and absorbing itself into the whole mind." (Kenneth Wuest, by paths in the Greek New Testament)

   B. *"Philos"*
   1. Friendship love
   2. Delight in
   3. Long for
   4. Do with pleasure

   C. *"Storgos"*
   1. Love for parents
   2. Husband for wife and wife for husband
   3. Family
   4. Used in Scripture in the negative sense "*astorgos*" is the opposite "without natural affection" Romans 1:31 / II Timothy 3:3

   D. *"Agapeo"*
   1. God-kind-of-love
   2. Esteems the one loved
   3. Gives unconditionally

II. **How does a disciple cultivate 'agape' kind of love?**

A. Matt. 22:36-40 - we must choose to love with a God-kind-of-love

    1. Jesus told us it is a commandment to love

    2. Matt. 22:36-40

    3. Because it is a command we choose to love first

    4. It is a willful (volitional) choice

B. We must have a pure heart to love with a God-kind-of-love

- What is a pure heart?
- I Tim. 1:5(a) / I Peter 1:27 / Matt. 24:12
- A heart free from immorality and past relationships
- A heart that has chosen to have eyes only for their mate
- Immorality blocks the ability to love freely and completely

C. We must have a clear conscience

- I Tim. 1:5(b) / Eph. 4:30-32 / Acts 24:16 (read this from the Amplified Version)
- What is a clear conscience?
- A heart free from bitterness, resentment and unforgiveness - these are like cancer to the love of a person
- The heart must be free from this pollution and defiling if it is to love completely
- Dr. Wuest translation of Acts 26:16

    "...herein do I exercise myself (constantly discipline myself)"

D. Faith unfeigned - genuine trust

- I Tim. 1:5(c)
- I Thess. 2:4 / Gal. 2:7 / I Tim. 1:11 / Acts 16:31
- What is genuine trust?
- Unmasked
- Without hypocrisy
- We must place our whole, uninhibited trust, confidence, reliance, upon God; this means becoming vulnerable, but you cannot love without it

A Disciple's Love Life – Student Handout

- Matthew 22:36-40
- John 13:34 / John 15:9-10
- I John 2:5 / I John 2:9-11 / I John 2:15-16 / I John 3:10-11 / I John 3:14-19
- I John 3:23 / I John 4:7-21

I. What are the four Greek words for love?

    A. _____

        1. _____

        2. _____

        3. "An over-mastering passion seizing upon and absorbing itself into the whole mind." (Kenneth Wuest, by paths in the Greek New Testament)

    B. _____

    C. _____

Used in Scripture in the negative sense "*astorgos*" is the opposite "without natural affection" Romans 1:31 / II Timothy 3:3

D. _____

_____

_____

_____

II. **How does a disciple cultivate 'agape' kind of love?**

A. Matt. 22:36-40 - we must _____ to love with a God-kind-of-love

_____

_____

_____

B. _____

- I Tim. 1:5(a) / I Peter 1:27 / Matt. 24:12

_____

_____

C. _____

- I Tim. 1:5(b) / Eph. 4:30-32 / Acts 24:16

_____

_____

_____

D. _____

- I Tim. 1:5(c)
- I Thess. 2:4 / Gal. 2:7 / I Tim. 1:11 / Acts 16:31

Notes

Living a Life Filled with Joy

Objective:

God wants His kids living filled with love. Love must have a conducive environment to grow and nurture.

- John 15:11 - the believer's joy is to be full
- John 17:13 - the believer is to have the full measure of Jesus' joy
- I Tim. 1:5 - purity and clear conscience
- Gal. 5:22 - joy, peace, etc. are qualities of love
- Rom. 14:17 - joy is a quality of the Kingdom
- Prov. 17:22 - joy does good like medicine
- Neh. 8:10 - joy is strength

The conclusion is clear - God wants His children to have joy and to laugh. What prevents us from a life filled with joy?

I. **Levels of the enemy's work**
   A. Oppression - harassment
   B. Suppression - stifles our emotions and ability to think
   C. Obsession - narrows our emotions, thinking and living experience
   D. Possession - controlled by Satan's kingdom

II. **How does Satan oppress?**
   A. He uses harassment of our mind, emotions and flesh
   B. He uses life experiences
      - hurts
      - injuries
      - offenses
      - broken families
   C. He will play on these in our mind and emotions
   D. He is seeking to suppress our emotions and mind
   E. We defeat these by:
      1. Exposing every thought to God and His Word
      2. Replacing the thoughts with the Word of God
      3. Declaring and affirming our position in Christ

III. **How does Satan suppress?**
   A. He tries to stifle our emotions so we cannot enjoy God's blessings

B. He works within our thinking

C. We defeat these by:

1. Taking every thought captive;

2. Exercising the blood of Jesus;

3. Exercising who we are in Christ;

4. Celebrating who we are in Christ and our victory;

IV. **How does Satan obsess?**

A. He takes control of our mind, will and emotions

B. We are held prisoner by the area he controls in our life

C. We can lose hope and even give up because we believe it will never change

D. We can actually remove our self if we let it go too far

E. How do we defeat these?

1. Go back to the place where we resisted God's grace

2. Take down the stronghold and give Jesus lordship and jurisdiction

3. Replace every thought

4. Declare who we are in Christ

F. Make it a personal study - "Who we are in Christ" and "Our identity in Christ"

1. Begin with Matthew and study through the New Testament

2. Mark the verses and make a list of the statements declaring our identity and our position in Jesus Christ

Living a Life Filled with Joy – Student Handout

Objective:

God wants His kids living filled with love. Love must have a conducive environment to grow and nurture.

- John 15:11 - the believer's joy is to be full
- John 17:13 - the believer is to have the full measure of Jesus' joy
- I Tim. 1:5 - purity and clear conscience
- Gal. 5:22 - joy, peace, etc. are qualities of love
- Rom. 14:17 - joy is a quality of the kingdom
- Prov. 17:22 - joy does good like medicine
- Neh. 8:10 - joy is strength

The conclusion is clear - God wants His children to have joy and to laugh. What prevents us from a life filled with joy?

II. Levels of the enemy's work

E. _____

F. _____

G. _____

H. _____

I.

II. How does Satan oppress?

A. _____

B. _____

C. _____

D. _____

E. _____

    1. _____

    2. _____

    3. _____

III. How does Satan suppress?

A. _____

B. _____

C. _____

    1. _____

    2. _____

    3. _____

    4. _____

IV. How does Satan obsess?

A. He takes _____

B. We are held prisoner by the area he controls in our life

C. We can lose hope and even give up because we believe it will never change

D. We can actually remove our self if we let it go too far

E. How do we defeat these?

1. _____

2. _____

3. _____

4. _____

F. Make it a personal study - _____

Notes

Discipleship is Being a Servant

I. **A disciple is a "follower" of Jesus**

    A. Matthew 4:19-22; Mark 1:16 - 20

        1. The call of Jonah and the Zebedee brothers

        2. "Follow Me"

        3. Strong's # 190 - *"akoloutheo"* - "to be in the same way with; i.e. to accompany"[24]

        4. Thayer's - "join as his attendant, cleave steadfastly, conform wholly to his example in living and if need be in dying also."[25]

    B. A scribe came to *"follow"* - Matt. 8:19-20

        1. He was a scribe a lawyer and expert in the Old Testament law

        2. He claimed he would follow (*akoloutheo*) where Jesus would lead

        3. Jesus said, "I live simply..."

        4. The man was looking for distinction and honor - the man lived for recognition

    C. A disciple with confused priorities was trying to "follow" - Matt. 8:21-22

        1. One who was already following Jesus wanted time for another urgent matter

        2. Jesus made an interesting statement to him

        3. He knew the man's heart was not really with Him

        4. You must be willing to make Jesus the number one priority

    D. A tax collector "follows" Jesus - Matt. 9:9

        1. He was a very successful and rich man hated by all Jews

        2. All gained by dishonesty and overtaxing people

        3. He left all of his wealth and riches to follow Jesus

        4. His heart changed

    E. Luke 5:11 gives the key point

        1. They forsook all

        2. Possessions, retirement, wealth and recreation cannot come first

---

[24] James Strong, S.T.D., LL.D., The Exhaustive Concordance of the Bible, Greek Dictionary of the New Testament, (New York, Nashville, 1890)

[25] Joseph Henry Thayer, D.D., Thayer's Greek-English Lexicon of the New Testament, (Grand Rapids, 1976)

3. They followed Him

4. His life became their pattern

II. **A disciple is called to live in humility**

A. How does God measure greatness in His kingdom? - Matt. 18:1-4

B. Matt. 23:1-12 - do not seek positions and titles

C. Matt. 9:34; Luke 22:24-26 - do not seek power and control

D. Matt. 20:20-28 - two disciples learn the cost of "following"

1. Drink My cup and lay down your life

2. The needs of people before your own life

3. Authority comes from serving

4. Honor comes from giving

III. **A disciple is called to be a servant**

A. Romans 6:15-20

1. A *"doulos"* slave - the most abject, servile slave in the Greek culture

2. We were once slaves to Satan and sin and had no will of our own

3. But we have changed masters

4. We are now servants of Christ whom we serve out of love and worship

B. Born a slave

1. Born a slave

2. We were born a slave to sin and Satan by our old nature

3. We are born again with a new nature

4. We no longer provide opportunities for sin and wrong doing

C. A slave whose will is for the master only

1. "One whose will is swallowed up in the will of another" (*Wuest*)

2. They live to serve their master alone

3. We once served Satan at all costs and detriment to our life

4. Now we serve the Lord Jesus Christ for freedom and abundant life

- D. A slave works for the interest of the master alone
    1. They serve with disregard to their own interest
    2. We once served Satan and sin because we were bound, though we may have wanted to be free
    3. Now we serve the Lord Jesus Christ and deny our own wants and interests because we love Him and He has our best interest at His heart.
- E. A slave served till death[26]
    1. They are only released by death.
    2. A sinner is free from his slavery only by death - then they serve in hell
    3. The believer gladly takes up his cross and follows His master even to death
    4. Death means eternal life with Jesus in heaven

---

[26] The information for points B-E are taken from "Romans in the Greek New Testament", by Kenneth Wuest, pp. 109-110

Discipleship is Being a Servant – Student Handout

I. A disciple is a "follower" of Jesus

   A. Matthew 4:19-22; Mark 1:16 - 20

   - Strong's # 190 - *"akoloutheo"* - "to be in the same way with; i.e. to accompany"[27]

   - Thayer's - "join as his attendant, cleave steadfastly, conform wholly to his example in living and if need be in dying also."[28]

   B. A _____ *"follow"*

   - Matt. 8:19-20 _____

   _____

   C. A disciple _____ *"follow"* -

   Matt. 8:21-22 _____

   _____

   D. A tax collector "follows" Jesus - Matt. 9:9

   _____

   _____

---

[27] James Strong, S.T.D., LL.D., The Exhaustive Concordance of the Bible, Greek Dictionary of the New Testament, (New York, Nashville, 1890)

[28] Joseph Henry Thayer, D.D., Thayer's Greek-English Lexicon of the New Testament, (Grand Rapids, 1976)

E. Luke 5:11 gives the key point

II. A disciple is called to live in humility

D. How does God measure greatness in His kingdom? - Matt. 18:1-4

E. Matt. 23:1-12 – _____

F. Matt. 9:34; Luke 22:24-26 - _____

D. Matt. 20:20-28 - _____

III. A disciple is called to be a servant

A. Romans 6:15-20

B. _____

C. _____

- 88 -

D. _____

E. _____

Notes

Me and My Tongue

Introduction:

James 3:1-12 gives amazing instruction regarding spiritual maturity and the measure by which a mature Christian is judged.

- Teachers are to be judged more strictly than those who are not teachers.
- Someone who does not have fault in the manner in which he uses his tongue is mature and able to discipline and control the whole body.

Did you catch those two amazing disciplines?

Then James says:

- One can train horses to obey
- One can guide ships over long voyages of the ocean.
- The tongue causes great fires, even death to some.
- One cannot seem to train the tongue. Out of it comes bitter and sweet at the same time.

How can one train the tongue? It takes great discipline and care. See it as a life long journey, not something for next month or next fall.

I. Instructions regarding the tongue.

   A. Jesus teaching on the tongue. - Matthew 12:32-37

      1. Do not blaspheme the Holy Spirit

      2. Make the tree good or make it evil - not both.

      3. Out of the abundance of the heart the mouth speaks.

      4. By your words you are justified or condemned.

   B. The disciples teaching on the tongue.

      1. James 1:26 - if you do not bridle your tongue you are deceiving yourself and your faith is in vain.

      2. James 4:11 - when you speak evil of your brother you are judging the law of God.

      3. Colossians 4:6 - seek to always season your speech with salt, by speaking with grace so you will know how to answer.

      4. When you refrain your lips from speaking evil and guile, you will love life and see good all the days of your life.

II. **Misuse of the tongue and the consequences.**

Read these aloud in class and discuss them:

Proverbs 12:8	Proverbs 26:24, 25
Proverbs 19:5	Proverbs 17:4
Proverbs 19:9	Proverbs 17:20
Proverbs 25:18	

III. **Wise use of the tongue and its blessing**

Proverbs 16:10	Proverbs 15:4
Proverbs 16:13	Proverbs 16:1
Proverbs 16:21	Proverbs 18:21
Proverbs 16:23-24	Proverbs 25:15
Proverbs 16:27-28	Proverbs 21:23
Proverbs 15:2	Proverbs 28:23

Me and My Tongue – Student Handout

How can one train the tongue? It takes great discipline and care. See it as a life long journey, not something for next month or next fall.

I.   Instructions regarding the tongue.

    A. Jesus teaching on the tongue. - Matthew 12:32-37

    _____

    _____

    _____

    _____

    B. The disciples teaching on the tongue.

        1. James   1:26   -
        _____

        2. James   4:11   -
        _____

        3. Colossians   4:6   -
        _____
        _____

II.   Misuse of the tongue and the consequences.

Read these aloud in class and discuss them:

Proverbs 12:8   Proverbs 26:24, 25

Proverbs 19:5   Proverbs 17:4
Proverbs 19:9   Proverbs 17:20
Proverbs 25:18

III.　Wise use of the tongue and its blessing

Proverbs 16:10   Proverbs 15:4
Proverbs 16:13   Proverbs 16:1
Proverbs 16:21   Proverbs 18:21
Proverbs 16:23-24   Proverbs 25:15
Proverbs 16:27-28   Proverbs 21:23
Proverbs 15:2   Proverbs 28:23

Notes

Living in The Power of a Clear Conscience

Examples of those who did not have a clear conscience:
- Gideon - *"Hello valiant warrior?"* - he had become bitter - Judges 6:1-12
- The sorcerer - Acts 8:18-24

I. What is a clear conscience?

A. Paul - Acts 24:16

1. Paul learned the value and power of a clear conscience
2. He disciplined himself to live in that power

B. A clear conscience is first toward God

- sins of commission (things we do that violate God's Word and command)
- sins of omission (things we do not do that we know we should be doing)
- we can be bitter toward God - *"Why did God let this happen"*

C. A clear conscience toward man

- Matt. 5:21-25
- "… they offend me"   -   "… I offend them"

D. "Toward man" - goes two ways

- Matt. 5:21-31 - if you offend them; if they offend you

II. How do you clear your conscience?

A. Recognize the root cause - Heb. 12:14-16

- rejecting grace
- repent of rejecting grace
- open your heart and accept grace
- accept it based upon the promise of God's eternal mercy

B. Release all accounts and judgments

C. Ask God to give you His heart and His eyes for the person

D. Accept responsibility for prayer and blessing them - Matt. 5:43-48

III. What is the power of a clear conscience?

A. Fullness of God's love – I Tim. 1:5

B. Freedom from debt - Matt. 6:10-14

C. Freedom from tormentors - Matt. 18:35

Living in The Power of a Clear Conscience – Student Handout

I. What is a clear conscience?

  A. Paul - Acts 24:16

  _____

  _____

  B. A clear conscience is first toward God

  - _____

  - _____

  - _____

  C. A clear conscience toward man - Matt. 5:21-25

  - _____   - _____

  D. "Toward man" - goes two ways - Matt. 5:21-31 - if you offend them; if they offend you

II. How do you clear your conscience?

  A. Recognize the root cause - Heb. 12:14-16

  - _____   - _____

  - _____   - _____

B. Release all accounts and judgments

_____

C. Ask God to give you His heart and His eyes for the person

_____

D. Accept responsibility for prayer and blessing them

- Matt. 5:43-48 - _____

III. What is the power of a clear conscience?

D. Fullness of God's love –I Tim. 1:5

_____

E. Freedom from debt - Matt. 6:10-14

_____

F. Freedom from tormentors - Matt. 18:35

_____

Notes

A Key to Great Faith...Understanding Authority

Introduction: - Luke 7:6-8 - great faith is connected with understanding authority. Why?

I. **The basis of authority**

   A. God's Kingdom is where His throne is established

   1. God's Kingdom is where His throne is and His throne is His authority. Where God's authority is invoked – that's where His throne is and His Kingdom is established.
   2. Jesus prayed "...*Thy Kingdom come...*" in Matt. 6:10
   3. Ps. 9:4-10; 97:1-2; 103:19 - God's throne on earth
   4. Ps. 11:4; Matt. 5:34 - God's throne in heaven
   5. Ps. 45:6-9; Heb. 1:8-12 - God's throne is forever
   6. We can bring God's throne and authority to earth today through prayer

   B. God's authority created all things

   1. Is. 66:1
   2. Heb. 1:3; 11:3; John 1:1-2
   3. Is. 40:12-31
   4. I Sam. 2:8; Ps. 24:1; 50:12; 89:11

   C. All authority has its origin in God and His throne

   1. Matt. 28:19
   2. Col. 2:9-10
   3. Romans 13:1
   4. Romans 13:2 - when a person resists authority they are resisting God

II. **God chose to delegate His authority through four arenas**

   A. Government

   1. Rom. 3:1-7 - God has established rulers and we are to honor them
   2. I Sam. 8:8, 9; 15:1 - God set forth the king over Israel
   3. I Sam. 16:1, 13 - God chose David to be king and set him forth
   4. Dan. 4:25, 26 - God made Nebuchadnezzar king of Babylon
   5. Is. 44:28; 45:1 - Cyrus chosen by God to be king
   6. Gen. 9:6; Num. 35:15-34; Deut. 25:1 - civil authority given by God

   B. Family

1. Gen. 118:18, 19 - "he shall command his children and his household after him..."
2. Num. 30:3-5 - authority of a father over His daughter's vows
3. Deut. 6:6-9 - home for teaching and training
4. I Cor. 11:3-12 - divine order of authority in the home
5. Eph. 5:21-33; Col. 3:18, 19 - role of each in the home
6. Ex. 20:12; Eph. 6:1-4; Col. 3:20, 21 - authority of parents in the home

C. Church
1. I Cor. 12:28 - God set governments in the church
2. Acts 15:1-3, 25-28 - authority of the apostles and elders
3. Acts 20:17, 28-31 - God had given oversight of the flock at Ephesus to the elders
4. Acts 6:1-7 - apostles appoint/give authority to deacons to do ministry in the church
5. Titus 1:5 - the ordaining of elders in every city
6. I Tim. 3:1-16 (*note vs.15 - that you may know how you ought to behave yourself in the house of God which is the church*)
7. I Pet. 5:1-5 - elders are to take oversight of the flock of God and feed it with humility and a servant's heart. The younger are to submit to the leadership of the elders.
8. Heb. 13:7 - honor those who feed you and have rule over you

D. Employer
1. Eph. 6:5-9 - authority of the employer over the employee
2. Col. 3:22-25 - do it as unto the Lord and not unto men

III. **God assigned limits to each arena of authority**

A. Government
1. To provide protection for the population from civil disobedience - Rom. 13:2-5
2. To provide protection for the population from outside threats - Exodus 17:9-10; Numbers 10:9; 26:2
3. To provide protection in civil matters, health, building, business (several passages in Exodus, Leviticus, Numbers, Deuteronomy)
4. It was not to take religious matters into its jurisdiction - I Sam. 13:11-13 - Saul offering sacrifices; II Chr. 26:18, 19 - Uzziah offered incense on the altar

B. Home and family
1. Authority for teaching and training - Deut. 6:7; Gal. 4:2
2. Authority over marriages - Ex. 22:17; John 14:1-3; Matt. 24:36

3. Authority for discipline - Prov. 13:29; 22:6, 15; 23:13-14; 26:3; 29:15
4. A rebellious child is to be turned over to the civil authorities - Deut. 21:18-21
5. Ex. 20:12; Eph. 6:2-3 - long life vs. short life

C. Church
1. Matt. 18:15-18 - discipline
2. I Cor. 5:1-5 - turn over to Satan
3. II Cor. 2:6-10 - restore and forgive
4. I Cor. 6:1-8 - judge angels
5. Luke 10:18 - tread on serpents
6. Matt. 16:18-19 - knock down the gates of hell
7. John 14:14-15 - prayer
8. Mark 16:14-18
9. Acts 6:1-4 - deacons and elders

D. Special limits
1. I Peter 2:13-16
2. Government - rules over religion - Dan. 3:16-18
3. Religion restricted - Acts 5:29
4. Appeal - Dan. 1:8-21

IV. **Our responsibility to the four arenas of authority**

A. We must submit to these arenas
1. Romans 13:2-7 - they are ministers of God
2. If not we will suffer consequences
3. Pay our taxes (even to a corrupt government such as Rome)
4. Give honor - show proper respect
5. Is not a terror to the good (unless it has lost its salt)
6. For conscience sake

B. Consequences of not submitting
1. I Sam. 15:22-23
2. Rebellion, witchcraft
3. Stubbornness, iniquity, idolatry
4. Understand the umbrella of protection

A Key to Great Faith...Understanding Authority – Student Handout

Luke 7:6-8 - great faith is connected with _____

I. The basis of authority

   A. God's Kingdom _____

   1. God's Kingdom is where His throne is and His throne is His authority. Where God's authority is invoked – that's where His throne is and His Kingdom is established.
   2. Jesus prayed "...*Thy Kingdom come...*" in Matt. 6:10
   3. Ps. 9:4-10; 97:1-2; 103:19 - God's throne on earth
   4. Ps. 11:4; Matt. 5:34 - God's throne in heaven
   5. Ps. 45:6-9; Heb. 1:8-12 - God's throne is forever
   6. We can bring God's throne and authority to earth today through prayer

   B. God's authority _____

   1. Is. 66:1
   2. Heb. 1:3; 11:3; John 1:1-2
   3. Is. 40:12-31
   4. I Sam. 2:8; Ps. 24:1; 50:12; 89:11

   C. All authority _____

   1. Matt. 28:19
   2. Col. 2:9-10
   3. Romans 13:1
   4. Romans 13:2 - when a person resists authority they are resisting God

II. **God chose to delegate His authority through four arenas**

   A. _____

   1. Rom. 3:1-7 - God has established rulers and we are to honor them
   2. I Sam. 8:8, 9; 15:1 - God set forth the king over Israel
   3. I Sam. 16:1, 13 - God chose David to be king and set him forth
   4. Dan. 4:25, 26 - God made Nebuchadnezzar king of Babylon
   5. Is. 44:28; 45:1 - Cyrus chosen by God to be king
   6. Gen. 9:6; Num. 35:15-34; Deut. 25:1 - civil authority given by God

   B. _____

   1. Gen. 118:18, 19 - "he shall command his children and his household after him..."
   2. Num. 30:3-5 - authority of a father over His daughter's vows
   3. Deut. 6:6-9 - home for teaching and training
   4. I Cor. 11:3-12 - divine order of authority in the home
   5. Eph. 5:21-33; Col. 3:18, 19 - role of each in the home
   6. Ex. 20:12; Eph. 6:1-4; Col. 3:20, 21 - authority of parents in the home

   C. _____

   1. I Cor. 12:28 - God set governments in the church
   2. Acts 15:1-3, 25-28 - authority of the apostles and elders
   3. Acts 20:17, 28-31 - God had given oversight of the flock at Ephesus to the elders
   4. Acts 6:1-7 - apostles appoint/give authority to deacons to do ministry in the church
   5. Titus 1:5 - the ordaining of elders in every city
   6. I Tim. 3:1-16 (*note vs.15 - that you may know how you ought to behave yourself in the house of God which is the church*)
   7. I Pet. 5:1-5 - elders are to take oversight of the flock of God and feed it with humility and a servant's heart. The younger are to submit to the leadership of the elders.
   8. Heb. 13:7 - honor those who feed you and have rule over you

   D. _____

1. Eph. 6:5-9 - authority of the employer over the employee
2. Col. 3:22-25 - do it as unto the Lord and not unto men

III. God assigned limits to each arena of authority

    A. _____

1. To provide protection for the population from civil disobedience - Rom. 13:2-5
2. To provide protection for the population from outside threats - Exodus 17:9-10; Numbers 10:9; 26:2
3. To provide protection in civil matters, health, building, business (several passages in Exodus, Leviticus, Numbers, Deuteronomy)
4. It was not to take religious matters into its jurisdiction - I Sam. 13:11-13 - Saul offering sacrifices; II Chr. 26:18, 19 - Uzziah offered incense on the altar

    B. _____

1. Authority for teaching and training - Deut. 6:7; Gal. 4:2
2. Authority over marriages - Ex. 22:17; John 14:1-3; Matt. 24:36
3. Authority for discipline - Prov. 13:29; 22:6, 15; 23:13-14; 26:3; 29:15
4. A rebellious child is to be turned over to the civil authorities - Deut. 21:18-21
5. Ex. 20:12; Eph. 6:2-3 - long life vs. short life

    C. _____

1. Matt. 18:15-18 - discipline
2. I Cor. 5:1-5 - turn over to Satan
3. II Cor. 2:6-10 - restore and forgive
4. I Cor. 6:1-8 - judge angels
5. Luke 10:18 - tread on serpents
6. Matt. 16:18-19 - knock down the gates of hell
7. John 14:14-15 - prayer
8. Mark 16:14-18
9. Acts 6:1-4 - deacons and elders

    D. _____

1. I Peter 2:13-16
2. Government - rules over religion - Dan. 3:16-18
3. Religion restricted - Acts 5:29
4. Appeal - Dan. 1:8-21

IV. Our responsibility to the four arenas of authority

A. We must _____

   Romans 13:2-7 -

   _____

   _____

   _____

   _____

   _____

B. _____

   I Sam. 15:22-23

   _____

   _____

   _____

Notes

Made in the USA
Middletown, DE
27 March 2017